STORNOWAY PRIMARY
WESTERN ISLES LIBRARIES

Readers are requested to take great care of the books while in their possession, and to point out any defects that they may notice in them to the Librarian.

This book is issued for a period of twenty-one days and should be returned on or before the latest date stamped below, but an extension of the period of loan may be granted when desired.

DATE OF RETURN	DATE OF RETURN	DATE OF RETURN

THE FACE OF THE EARTH

THE WASTE LANDS

TESSA POTTER

Editorial planning
Jollands Editions

MACMILLAN
EDUCATION

© Macmillan Education Limited 1987
© BLA Publishing Limited 1987

First published 1987
Reprinted 1987

Published by
MACMILLAN EDUCATION LTD
Houndmills, Basingstoke, Hampshire RG21 2XS
and London
Companies and representatives
throughout the world

Designed and produced by BLA Publishing Limited,
Swan Court, East Grinstead, Sussex, England.

Also in LONDON · HONG KONG · TAIPEI · SINGAPORE · NEW YORK

A Ling Kee Company

Illustrations by Kevin Diaper, Pat Harby/Linden Artists,
 Brian Watson/Linden Artists, Phil Weare/Linden Artists,
 and BLA Publishing Limited
Colour origination by Chris Willcock Reproductions
Printed in Hong Kong

British Library Cataloguing in Publication Data

Potter, Tessa
 The waste lands. — (The face of the earth)
 — (Macmillan world library)
 1. Deserts — Juvenile literature
 I. Title   II. Series
 551.4   GB611

ISBN 0-333-42629-0
ISBN 0-333-42620-7 Series

Acknowledgements
**The Publishers wish to thank the following
organizations for their invaluable assistance in the
preparation of this book.**

British Petroleum
Canadian High Commission
Oxfam

Photographic credits
t = top b = bottom l = left r = right

cover: ZEFA

4 ZEFA; 5 Ed Lawrenson; 6 The Hutchison Library; 7,
8 ZEFA; 8/9 Hans Christian Heap/Seaphot; 9 The
Hutchison Library; 15*t* Canadian High Commission; 15*b*
John Lythgoe/Seaphot; 16 L.H. Newman/NHPA; 17
Stephen Krasemann/NHPA; 19 Jonathan Chester/NHPA;
20*t* The Hutchison Library; 20*b* Jeremy Hartley/Oxfam;
21 Douglas Dickens; 22 Peter Johnson/NHPA; 23*t* The
Hutchison Library; 23*b* Peter Scoones/Seaphot; 26, 27*t*
ZEFA; 27*b*, 28 The Hutchison Library; 29*t*, 29*b* ZEFA;
30 Vincent Serventy/Seaphot; 31*t*, 31*b* The Hutchison
Library; 32 Hans Christian Heap/Seaphot; 33 ZEFA; 34
The Hutchison Library; 35 British Petroleum; 36, 37 The
Hutchison Library; 38 British Petroleum; 39 Ed
Lawrenson; 40 Dennis Firminger/Seaphot; 41*t* ZEFA;
41*b* Hans Christian Heap/Seaphot; 43*t*, 43*b* Jeremy
Hartley/Oxfam; 44 ZEFA; 45*t* The Hutchison Library;
45*b* Mike Coltman/Seaphot

Note to the reader
In this book there are some words in the text which are printed in **bold** type. This shows that the
word is listed in the glossary on page 46. The glossary gives a brief explanation of words which may
be new to you.

Contents

Introduction

▼ It is very dry in the desert. Not many plants can grow there except coarse grass. This is the Kara Kum Desert in the USSR.

All over the world there are huge areas of waste land. These are places where almost nothing lives. These waste lands are so deserted that we call them deserts. Deserts are either very hot or very cold. They have very little rain.

Deserts are too dry for most plants and crops to grow, so it is very difficult for animals and people to live there. Some plants and animals do survive in these unfriendly, **hostile** places. A few people have also learned how to live in deserts.

The way desert people live has not changed for hundreds of years.

Today, some people go to work there because the waste lands are rich in oil and valuable **minerals**. These are needed for many **industries** all over the world. The deserts are being changed by the people who live and work in them now.

The desert lands may be spoiled for the future if we are not careful to keep the balance between the old and new ways of life.

4

Hot deserts

Look at the map on pages 24 and 25. You will see that the largest hot desert in the world is the Sahara Desert in Africa. It is very hot there during the day. It becomes cold at night as the desert cools down.

All the hot deserts of the world are covered in sand, rock and small stones. They have less than 25 cm of rain in one year. It is difficult for plants to grow because of this. The desert people who live there are called **nomads**. They move from place to place to find food and water for themselves and their animals.

▼ Scientists and other people visit Antarctica and work there. They travel over the snow on skidoos. These are like motor cycles. They have belts which bite into the snow instead of wheels.

Cold deserts

There are cold deserts around the North and South Poles, on the waste lands of the Arctic and Antarctic. These deserts are always covered by snow and ice. The water is nearly always frozen and cannot be used by plants and animals.

The land to the south of the Arctic Ocean is called **tundra**. There the snow melts for a few weeks each summer. During this short time, plants can grow and provide food for animals. A few nomads live on the tundra all year round.

There are other cold deserts in the high mountains of central Asia and South America. These deserts, like the Gobi Desert in Mongolia, have freezing cold winters, but hot summers.

How deserts are made

wind

PACIFIC
OCEAN

Rocky Mountains

Winds which blow from the Pacific Ocean rise when they reach the Rocky Mountains. The moisture in the air falls as rain. By the time the air reaches the other side of the mountains it is dry. There is no more rain to fall. This is how a rain shadow desert is made.

Deserts are made in parts of the world where there is not enough water for many plants to grow. Around the edges of some of the hot deserts is land which is known as **semi-desert**. In the semi-desert there is just enough rain for small trees and plants to grow. Plants stop the soil from breaking up and blowing away. Some nomadic people keep herds of cattle there. The cattle feed on the plants. If too many animals strip the land of plants, the soil blows away. Then nothing can grow so the land turns into desert.

Very old paintings have been found on rocks in the Sahara Desert. These show that 10 000 years ago, people kept cows in parts of the Sahara that are now desert. There must have been grass to feed the cows. The cattle may have stripped the land and the area turned into desert.

▼ **This rock painting was found in the Tassili Mountains in the Sahara Desert. It shows that 10 000 years ago cattle grazed on land that is now desert.**

Deserts and the sea

Most of the largest deserts are found a long way from the sea. Winds pick up **moisture** as they blow across the sea. When the winds reach the land this moisture falls as rain. By the time the winds have blown a long way inland they are almost dry. Very little rain falls, so some places a long way from the sea become deserts.

rain shadow desert

▼ In Antarctica rain falls as snow. It is blown by the wind and snow drifts are formed. These heap up and add to the ice-cap.

Deserts and mountains

When winds blow off the sea and reach mountains the clouds are pushed upwards. This makes the clouds drop their rain. The land on the side of the mountains nearest the sea can get a lot of rain. The land on the other side of the mountains gets very little rain. It becomes a desert. It is called a **rain shadow** desert. This is how the Rocky Mountains helped to make the Great American Desert.

Deserts near the sea

Deserts are also found near the sea. On the west coast of South America there is the Atacama Desert and on the west coast of southern Africa there is the Namib Desert. In these places the air is calm and there is very little wind. Warm winds blow gently over the cold water near these coasts. The moisture in the air turns to mist and does not fall as rain.

The polar regions

The winds that blow over the Arctic and the Antarctic are very cold. They carry a little moisture which falls as snow. The snow helps to make the **ice-caps** of the North and South Poles.

Water and wind

Some deserts are thousands of years old. Others are quite young. The desert scene, or **landscape**, can change from one moment to another and from one desert to another. Some deserts are covered with sand. Other deserts are covered with rocks or stones. Some deserts are quite flat and others have hills and **valleys**.

Over thousands of years the weather changes the shape of deserts. When rain does fall, it falls in short, fierce storms. These storms wash away the top layer of soil and wear away, or **erode**, the rocks. The land becomes hard and dry. Rain water cannot sink quickly into the soil. Dry valleys, called **wadis**, can flood with water in a few minutes. Animals and people can drown in these floods.

Sand dunes

Wind helps to shape the landscape of the desert. It erodes the face of the land over many years. Strong winds whip up the sand and blow it from one place to another. In this way the landscape is changing all the time.

Sand is made from pieces of hard rock called **quartz**. The quartz has been worn down by the wind into tiny grains of sand. The wind blows the sand across the desert into huge piles called sand **dunes**. Some dunes in the Sahara are 400 m high. The sand dunes change their shape and size as the wind changes its direction and strength.

▲ This wadi in Morocco is almost dry. It may stay dry for months or even years. When it does rain, it rains heavily and the wadi fills quickly with fast-flowing water.

▶ These huge sand dunes in the Arabian Desert have been shaped by the wind. Their sizes and shapes are always changing.

▲ In the Navajo National Monument, USA, huge pillars of rock point to the sky. They are all that is left of hills worn away by the wind and the sand.

The Great American Desert

Water and wind have shaped the landscape of the Great American Desert over thousands of years. River water mixed with pebbles and sand has carved deep valleys, called **canyons**, through the rocks.

Sand is a powerful tool in shaping desert landscapes. Sand blown by high winds has cut and carved the rocks into strange shapes. The soft parts of the rock are worn away first by the tiny grains of sand. Then pieces of harder rock may break away too. In Monument Valley, Arizona, USA, the strange, flat-topped hills are made of very hard stone. The softer rock around them has all been worn away.

In the desert, sand blown by the wind can wear away the bottom of wooden poles carrying telephone wires. Metal shields are put around the poles to protect the wood. The poles only last a few years.

9

Plants in hot deserts

Plants make their own food from sunlight, soil and water. In the hot desert there is too much sun but not enough water. Months, or even years, may pass between one shower of rain and the next. Then the sun, blazing down from above, quickly dries the desert.

The desert plantlife, on which the animals depend, has **adapted** to this lack of water. Two groups of plants have their own ways of living in the hot desert. One group, like the desert poppy, will only burst into life after a heavy fall of rain. The other group, like the cactus, stays alive and goes on growing year after year.

Waiting for water

After a heavy storm the desert plants that have been waiting for water burst into life. They flower for a short time and then die, leaving their seeds in the desert soil. The seeds that are not eaten by animals lie **dormant** in the sand. They do not start growing until it rains again, which may not be for several years.

A light shower of rain is not enough to make the seeds grow. If they started growing after a light shower, there would not be enough water for them. The plants would not flower and make new seeds. The seeds have a hard coat which only becomes soft and **dissolves** after a heavy fall of rain. The desert is covered with a carpet of flowers after a heavy rainstorm.

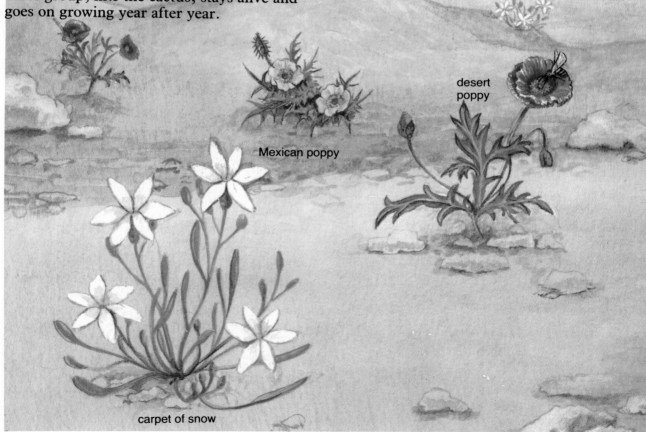

Mexican poppy

desert poppy

carpet of snow

Storing water

Some plants stay alive in the hot desert by storing water. These plants are called **succulents**. The best known of these juicy plants is the cactus. Many types of cactus are found in the Great American Desert.

After a rainstorm, cacti soak up water through their giant roots. They store this water in their barrel-like stems. The giant saguaro (*sag-u-ro*) cactus can store hundreds of litres of water in this way.

Cacti have very prickly spines instead of leaves. The spines do not lose a lot of water in the heat. They help to protect the cacti from birds, animals and even people who need their water. The giant cactus can stay alive or over 200 years.

saguaro cactus

barrel cactus

aloe

Wildlife in hot deserts

Insects are found in all the hot deserts of the world. They can feed on live or dead plants. Birds and small animals are also able to survive though food is scarce. They feed on plants, seeds and insects. Life is full of danger for the plant-eaters. There are larger meat-eating animals in the desert waiting to pounce on them and eat them.

All desert animals, large and small, must be able to live with very little water. They also have to find ways of keeping cool in the burning desert heat.

Reptiles

Reptiles are **cold-blooded** animals. This means that their bodies are hot or cold depending on the weather. They cannot make their own heat. In the hottest part of the day reptiles have to find ways of keeping cool.

Lizards are reptiles that find shade in burrows, between rocks or under plants. They have webbed or scaly feet which are good for running fast over hot sand. They get most of the water they need from the plants and insects they eat.

gila woodpecker

jack rabbit

roadrunner bird

diamond backed rattlesnake

kangaroo rat

Small animals

Other animals are **warm-blooded**. This means that they can keep their bodies at a steady temperature. Warm-blooded animals can make their own heat. They can keep their bodies cool by panting or sweating, but they use up precious water when they do so. During the day, they have to shelter from the hot sun.

Kangaroo rats live in burrows under the sand. They come out at night to look for food. They use their long back legs for jumping over the hot sand, and to escape from their enemies. Sometimes they are caught and eaten by the desert kit fox.

Birds

Birds find it easier to survive than animals. They can fly away from their enemies and find shade from the hot sun. The gila woodpecker pecks holes in cacti to make its nest and to find food and water. These holes also give shelter to small elf owls. The roadrunner bird cannot fly but it has long legs. It can run fast over the hot sand.

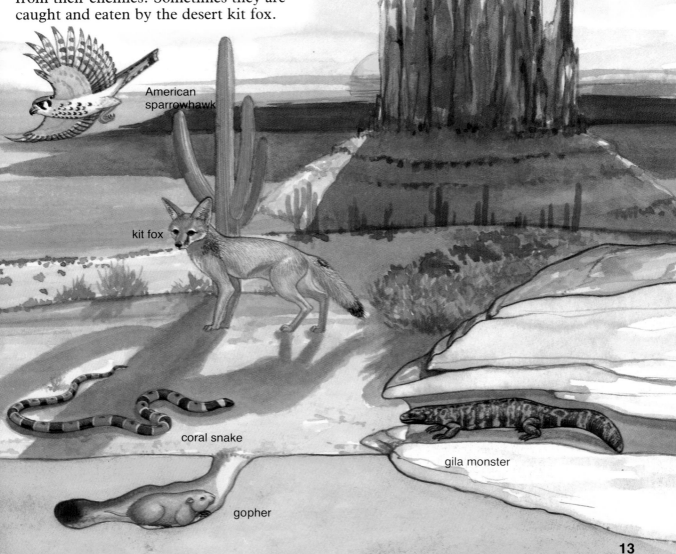

American sparrowhawk

kit fox

coral snake

gopher

gila monster

The tundra

The cold dry waste lands near the North Pole are called the tundra. This name comes from a Finnish word which means 'barren land'. The tundra is 'barren' because no trees or crops can grow there. The winters are long and cold. Snow covers the ground for more than half the year. The summers are short and there is very little rain.

Tundra covers one-tenth of all the land on Earth. The Arctic tundra stretches along a wide **belt** of land between the ice-cap of the North Pole and the northern pine forests of Greenland, Alaska, Canada, Europe and USSR.

The landscape

During the **Ice Age** a huge sheet of ice covered the tundra. This ice-cap melted and left the ground flat, with patches of rock and little soil. The tundra is frozen hard and covered in snow from September to April or May. The summer sun melts only the top few centimetres of frozen soil. During this time the ground is wet and boggy.

One metre below the surface the soil is frozen all the time. This soil is called **permafrost**. The permafrost stops water from draining away.

▼ The tundra is a cold, mostly flat, belt of land where large trees cannot grow. It lies between the Arctic ice-cap and the line where trees are able to grow. This is known as the tree line.

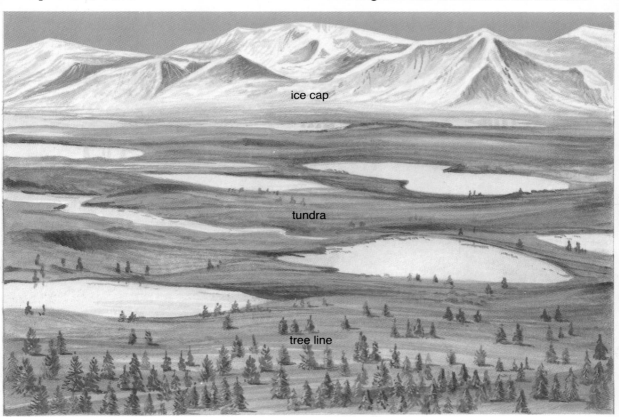

ice cap

tundra

tree line

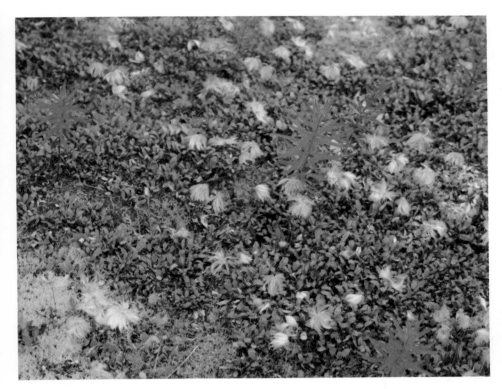

◄ On the tundra, the snow melts for a few weeks in the short summer. Then the land is covered with a carpet of beautiful flowers. These bloom for a few weeks only and then die.

▼ These lichens and mosses are growing in the tundra near Frobisher Bay in northern Canada.

Plant life

Many types of plant grow on the tundra. They are short and grow close to the ground to protect them from the cold harsh winds. **Lichens** and **mosses** cover the rocks. These plants can stay alive under the snow during the winter.

Some plants flower when the snow melts. Beautiful Arctic poppies, buttercups, bright marsh marigolds and rock plants bloom for a short time. These plants die down each year during the freezing winter months.

Grasses and heathers grow on flat stony ground. In some places animal droppings make the soil richer and low bushes and shrubs can grow. Small trees, such as the Arctic willow, grow in very sheltered places. They grow only 10 cm high but spread a long way over the ground. No large trees grow on the tundra. The permafrost stops their roots going deep into the earth.

Wildlife in the tundra

Many animals live off the plants which grow on the tundra. Large plant-eating animals are the caribou and the musk-ox. Lemmings and voles are small plant-eaters. All of these animals provide food for **predators**. Predators are meat-eating animals. They kill and eat other animals. The fierce Arctic wolf hunts the caribou and musk-ox. The Arctic fox eats small lemmings and voles.

Many insects also live on the tundra. During the cold winter they survive as eggs, or **larvae**. Spiders, bees and even butterflies hatch out in the warm weather. The tundra comes alive with mosquitoes which breed on the marshes and bogs. They provide food for the many birds which fly in during the summer months. Only the snowy owl and ptarmigan (*tar-mi-gan*) stay on the tundra all year.

Keeping warm

How do these animals keep warm and survive during the cold winter months? Some animals, such as the Arctic fox and musk-ox, have very long hair and thick fur skins, or **pelts**. This thick fur stops their body heat from escaping.

◄ The Arctic fox is well adapted to surviving in the cold Arctic waste lands. The furry coat, and tufts of hair growing inside the ears, help to keep the animal warm.

The skin around the ears and noses of these northern animals is usually hairy. The Arctic fox has thick tufts of hair inside its ears. The long coat of the musk-ox comes right down to its feet. The ptarmigan even has feathers on the soles of its feet! In winter the lemmings and voles dig tunnels under the snow to keep warm.

Moving around

Caribou have broad hoofs and travel easily over ice and soft snow. They use their hoofs and antlers to scrape away the snow to find lichen and moss to eat. In winter they travel in herds and make long journeys south looking for food.

Musk-oxen also use their hoofs to scrape away the snow in winter. They have a special way of protecting their young calves from the fierce cold and from predators. The bulls, the male oxen, make a ring around the cows and young calves. The bulls charge any wolf who dares to attack.

▶ Musk-oxen have a good way of protecting their calves against cold winds and fierce predators. They stand in a circle around the calves to protect them.

▲ Musk-oxen roam the tundra in herds. They feed on mosses and lichens. Their long shaggy coats protect them from the cold.

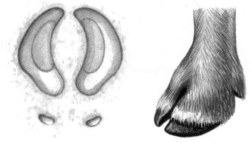

▲ The wide hoof print of the caribou (*left*), and the strong hoof of the musk ox (*right*) show how animals can move easily over soft snow.

The ends of the Earth

narwhals

polar bear

walrus

harbour seals

The frozen waste lands around the North Pole and the South Pole are known as the polar regions. They are the coldest places on Earth and are covered by enormous caps of ice. Although we think of these two regions as being much the same as each other, they are quite different.

The Arctic is a large frozen ocean surrounded by the most northern lands of North America, Europe, and the USSR. Antarctica is the **continent** around the South Pole. It is a frozen mass of land surrounded by the sea. The Arctic is frozen water surrounded by land, but the Antarctic is frozen land surrounded by water.

▲ Polar bears are the largest of the Arctic predators. They feed on seals and young walruses. The narwhals feed on fish and squid.

Life in the Arctic

A few people live on the Arctic waste land. These include the Inuit (Eskimos), and the Saami (Lapps) of northern Finland. In the past, all these people were nomads. Since oil and minerals have been found in the Arctic regions their nomadic way of life has changed.

Amongst the animals that live in the Arctic, the polar bear is the most well known. It is the largest of all bears. Polar bears are fierce predators and hunt seals in the water around the drifting **pack ice**.

Thick coats of fur protect them from the cold as they swim in the icy water. The female bear digs a cave in the snow during the winter where her young are born.

Many kinds of seal live in the Arctic. The largest of these is the walrus. Walruses use their long tusks for digging clams and worms from the seabed.

Antarctica

The ice-cap in Antarctica is higher and colder than the Arctic ice-cap. In many places it is 2000 m deep. The ice only melts on the edges of the sea around this great mass of land. No people live there except scientists. They come from all over the world to study the wildlife and the weather.

Animals and birds stay close to the Antarctic coast. The seas are full of fish and tiny living things called **plankton**. These provide food for whales. Seals also feed on fish and plankton, but the fierce leopard seal eats penguins as well.

Penguins cannot fly. They use their short wings as flippers to swim in the sea and catch fish. The largest of these birds is the emperor penguin. The female lays her egg on the ice in the middle of winter. The male bird keeps the egg warm until the chick hatches out. He can carry the egg around on his feet!

▼ Around the Antarctic coastline different kinds of seals and penguins are found. These are rockhopper penguins. On the black sand is a group of male elephant seals.

Water in the hot desert

Desert plants and animals have adapted to living without much water. People who live in the desert need water every day to survive. The search for water shapes the lives of everyone in the desert.

People who visit the desert to drill for oil need at least seven litres of water a day for drinking, cooking and washing. The nomadic people who spend all their lives in the desert do not need this amount. They travel during the coolest part of the day, so their bodies do not use up as much water.

Finding water

Most water in the desert comes from sudden rainstorms. In some places, water from below the desert comes to the surface. This makes springs or water-holes.

Some nomads are always on the move trying to find fresh water for themselves and their animals. Other desert people

▲ Wind power can be used to bring water to the surface from deep under the ground. The water can then be stored in tanks. This type of well is called an Artesian well because it was first used in Artois in France.

survive by collecting and storing every drop of water they find. They are able to get water from damp sand or from under the ground. They suck up water with a hollow reed and store it in gourds or empty ostrich eggshells. These gourds and shells can be buried under the ground. The water in them can be used when there is a **drought**.

◄ Sometimes wells have been dug in the semi-desert where there is water beneath the ground. The villagers are collecting water in clay pots. The donkey will carry the pots back to the village.

▲ An oasis is a place in the desert where water comes to the surface. Trees and crops can grow. People can settle and make their homes there. This oasis is in Morocco.

Oases

In some parts of the desert there is enough water for people to stay in one place. This water comes from rocks far below the desert. It is rain water which has collected underground for thousands of years. In some places the water is forced up to the surface through breaks in the rocks.

Where the water comes to the surface of a desert, there is a green area called an oasis. The water makes the land **fertile**. People can grow crops there and keep animals. Oases have also been made where deep wells have been dug to find water beneath the desert.

Oases are a long way from other people and towns. The people who live at an oasis must provide nearly everything they need for themselves. The date palm can be used to make many things. The fruit provides food. The **sap** of the tree is made into wine. The tree trunks are used for firewood and to make shelter. The leaves are used for shelter and bedding too. The leaf **fibres** are made into rope. Crops can be grown in the shade of the trees. These include figs, apricots, maize, millet and sweet potatoes.

Survival in the hot desert

► This Saudi Arabian standing in front of his Bedouin tent shows how desert ways are changing. Apart from his traditional head veil, his clothes are more suitable for town life. He is holding a falcon. This bird is trained to hunt small birds and animals.

Most people who have learned to survive in the desert are nomads. There is not enough rain in the desert for them to stay in one place. They have to keep moving to find water and food. The plants which provide food for their animals can only grow where there is enough water.

Hunters and gatherers

The San (Bushmen) of the Kalahari Desert in Africa still hunt wild animals for food. They also gather plants and roots to eat. They travel in small family groups during the coolest part of the day. They wear very little clothing and have few **possessions**. The San have survived in this way for hundreds of years.

Nomadic herders

Most people who live in the desert are nomadic herders. The Bedouin, which means 'desert dwellers', have lived in the deserts of the Middle East and North Africa for over 2000 years. The Tuareg live in the Sahara and on the southern edge of the desert.

The Bedouin and the Tuareg were the first tribes to live in the Sahara. They both lead much the same way of life. They move from one oasis to another with herds of animals. Camels carry their tents and possessions. The camels also provide the nomads with milk and cheese. Camel dung is burned for cooking and heating. Camel hair is woven into cloth and made into tents or clothes.

◄ The San make their shelters from long grass and tree branches. In this group, one of them is seen stretching an antelope skin. They sell skins for any goods they need.

Comfortable clothes

People living in the desert need to keep cool during the day and to keep warm at night. The Tuareg and the Bedouin people wear long flowing robes. These robes hang loose during the heat of the day and help to keep people cool. They also cover the whole body and protect people from the sun. When the cool evening comes, people wrap the robes close to their bodies to keep warm. The Tuareg wear blue robes, while the Bedouin wear mostly white. Head veils can be wrapped around their faces to stop any blowing sand from entering their mouths and noses.

A new life

Many nomads are now giving up their old way of life. Some settle and become farmers. Many of the Bedouin have stopped travelling. They live and work at the oilfields in the desert.

These people are just about to leave their base camp for a trek in the Sinai Desert, Egypt. They use Landrovers to carry their frame tents and equipment.

Where are the waste lands?

About one-fifth of all the land on Earth has less than 25 cm of rain each year. A large part of this land is an almost continuous belt of desert. It stretches from the west coast of Africa through the Middle East to the Gobi Desert in Asia.

The hot deserts

In Death Valley in California the **temperature** once reached 57°C. It was hot enough to fry an egg on the rocks. The driest place in the world is found in the Atacama Desert of South America. It may not have rained there for 400 years. In parts of the Sahara there has been no rain for more than 11 years. In the north west of Queensland, Australia, there was no rain for 14 years. Children grew up without knowing what rain was like.

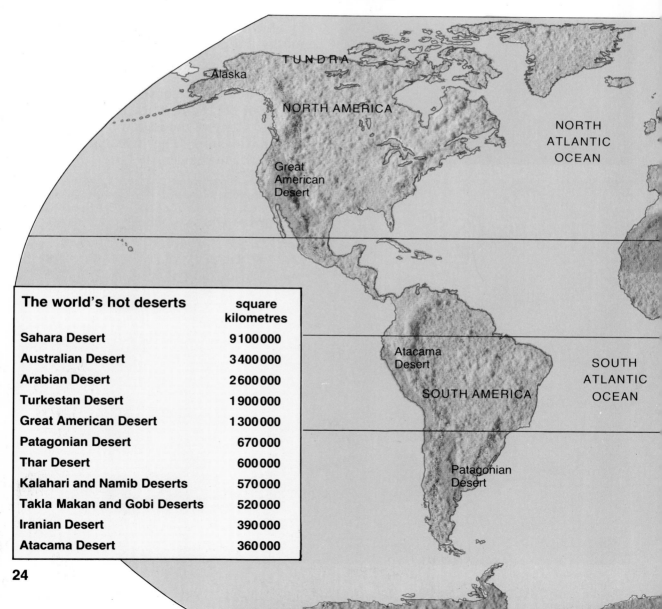

The world's hot deserts	square kilometres
Sahara Desert	9 100 000
Australian Desert	3 400 000
Arabian Desert	2 600 000
Turkestan Desert	1 900 000
Great American Desert	1 300 000
Patagonian Desert	670 000
Thar Desert	600 000
Kalahari and Namib Deserts	570 000
Takla Makan and Gobi Deserts	520 000
Iranian Desert	390 000
Atacama Desert	360 000

The Sahara in North Africa is the largest desert in the world. It is over nine million square kilometres.

The world's highest sand dunes are found in the Sahara Desert. They can be 430 m high.

The cold deserts

The cold deserts around the South and North Poles are the two coldest places on Earth. The coldest temperature ever recorded was at Vostok in Antarctica on 21 July 1983. It was −89.2°C. In Antarctica it is usually −60°C in winter. In the Arctic, in winter, the temperature often drops to −57°C. The average temperature is about −36°C.

The huge Antarctic ice-cap is 2000 m thick in some places. Nine-tenths of all the world's fresh water is frozen there. If the ice-cap should melt, the level of the seas would rise. Everything less than 65 m above sea-level would disappear under the water!

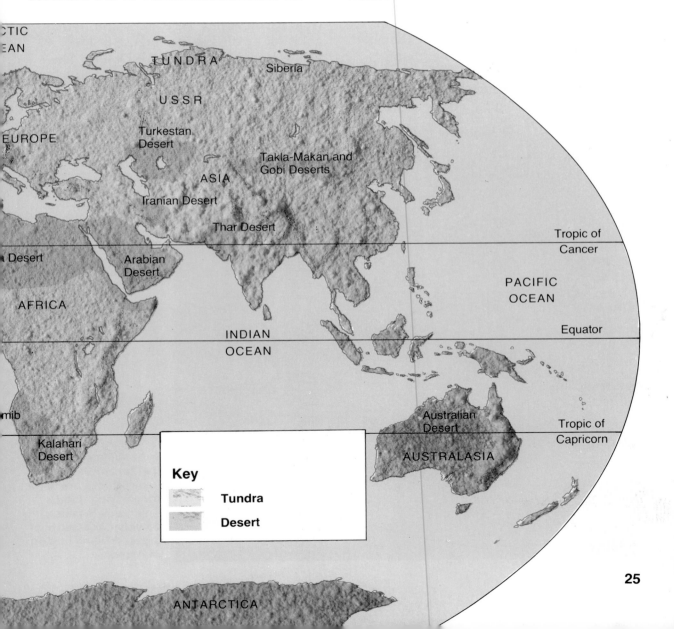

25

Desert barriers

To find new land and work, people have crossed many **barriers**. The sea, the mountains and the desert are all natural barriers. The desert has always been a hard and dangerous place to explore.

Before there were planes and cars, people had to cross the desert on foot, or ride on camels or donkeys. At one time nomads and a few explorers were the only people to cross the desert. The life of desert people did not change.

Valuable oil and minerals lie beneath some desert waste lands. The people who work at the mines need food, water and equipment. New roads and railways have to be made. Wherever this happens the desert people are affected and their way of life can change.

The Mojave Desert

Over one hundred years ago the dream of finding gold took many people into the deserts of California. Some crossed the Rocky Mountains on foot. Some people rode donkeys. They carried their food and water with them. This was the time of the Gold Rush. A few were lucky and found gold. Many died in the intense heat of Death Valley in the Mojave Desert. The wild donkeys, or burros, of the Mojave are descended from the donkeys brought to the desert by these first gold **prospectors**.

◄ Death Valley in the Californian Desert, USA, was well named. Many people died in this hot, dry desert in the Gold Rush over one hundred years ago.

► In some parts of the Sahara Desert, heavy trucks are used for carrying goods. This truck is taking on water and petrol at a desert filling station in Algeria.

► Camels have carried people and goods across the desert for hundreds of years. Camels can travel for very long distances without food and water.

Crossing the Sahara

The Sahara is a huge natural barrier across the continent of Africa. It is thought to be rich in oil and minerals. Many areas have not been searched for minerals. There are still only a few roads across the Sahara Desert.

The camel has been used to carry goods across the desert for hundreds of years. The camel of the Sahara is the single-humped dromedary (*drom-e-dar-ee*). It is well adapted to desert life. The large feet of the camel spread its weight over the loose sand. It can survive without water for quite a long time but it can drink up to 115 litres when water is available.

Camels are still used by the nomads of the Sahara to carry goods. The nomads travel with long **caravans** of camels, carrying salt from the southern Sahara. In parts of the Sahara, camels are gradually being replaced by trucks.

The cold deserts of Asia

The cold deserts of central Asia are the Takla Makan and the Gobi Desert. These deserts are still some of the least known parts of the world. They have no sea coast. Before there were planes, people had to make a long journey on foot or on horseback through Siberia or China.

The Gobi Desert

The Gobi Desert is in the southern part of Mongolia, near to China. It is a huge desert covered with sand, gravel and rocks. It has hot summers, but very cold winters. Icy winds from Siberia blow across the desert. The grass and patches of **scrub** provide food for wild horses and yaks. The yak is a kind of ox with a long shaggy coat.

The Mongols once ruled over large parts of Asia and Europe. They were very skilled horsemen. Today they use two-humped Bactrian camels to travel across the Gobi Desert. Some of the Mongol people are nomadic herders. They wander from one grazing place to another with their sheep, goats, yaks and horses. When their herds have eaten all the grass in one place, the Mongols move on to find fresh grass. They get milk, cheese, butter and meat from their animals. The Mongols make clothes from sheepskin and woollen cloth. Their tents, called **yurts**, are made with layers of thick **felt** and skin to keep out the cold wind.

Trucks are now being used to cross the Gobi Desert. During very cold winters the Mongols have to wrap their trucks in sheepskin to stop them from freezing. As in many waste lands of the world, some of these nomads have given up their old way of life.

These two-humped Bactrian camels are used by the nomads of the Gobi Desert. The camels' thick fur keeps out the bitter cold.

The Mongol people keep herds of sheep and goats. They have to keep the herd on the move in the search for fresh grass.

The Yakuts of Siberia

North-east Siberia is a cold treeless waste land. It is winter there for eight or nine months of the year. The country is covered with frozen bogs. It is home to a few nomadic people. The largest group are the Yakuts. They hunt and breed caribou and keep cattle and horses. They are also trappers and sell their furs to buy food and goods for the winter from the city of Yakutsk.

Scientists have developed a type of seed that is strong enough to survive in the ground in the winter and ripen quickly in the short summer. Now the Yakuts can grow their own crops, they are beginning to settle.

Siberia is very rich in gold and diamonds. There is also iron, coal and oil there. As more mines are opened and more oil is found, life is changing for the nomadic people who live there.

◄ Not so long ago, most of the Mongol people were nomads. They wandered through the Gobi Desert, living in their round tents, called yurts. Many of them now live in settlements, like this one near Ulan Bator in Mongolia. They still live in yurts.

The Australian Desert

About three-quarters of Australia is desert or semi-desert. This huge waste land lies at the centre of the country and is sometimes called the outback. Most Australians live around the coasts where there is enough rainfall for plants to grow.

When you move inland from the coasts towards the dry desert there are less and less plants. Eucalyptus (*you-ka-lip-tus*) and acacia (*a-kay-sha*) trees survive as belts of scrub, covering huge areas of land. It is so dry that there are often bush fires. The seeds of some plants have adapted to survive after fire.

Animals of the desert

The animals that live in these waste lands, like kangaroos and wallabies, are only found in Australia. In most parts of the world, mammal babies grow inside their mothers. In Australia the mammal baby is born very small and grows outside the mother, in a pouch. Mammals with pouches are called **marsupials**.

Another animal found only in Australia is the emu. It is a large bird that cannot fly but it can run very fast. The male bird is smaller than the female.

The first Australians

The first people to live in Australia were the **Aborigines**. They learned to survive in the desert. Like the San of the Kalahari Desert, the Aborigines were hunter gatherers. They hunted kangaroos and emus and gathered plants and berries for food.

The Aborigines knew all about the lands they lived in. They knew about plants and animals, and where to find water. Their wonderful legends and stories are still passed down to their children.

▼ These are grey kangaroos in front of a eucalyptus tree. With their huge back legs kangaroos leap quickly over the ground. One grey kangaroo is known to have made one leap over 13 m long.

▶ The Aborigines are great artists. This man is decorating a wooden shield. They often use tree bark to paint on. The patterns on their paintings have special meanings. Only the Aborigines know what they mean.

Working in the desert

When Europeans came to Australia, the Aborigines' way of life began to change. Their hunting lands became farms and **cattle stations**. Some of them now work on the stations as stockmen and live there in camps. Others work in the mines or in towns.

More and more people are going to the Australian Desert to work in the mines. Long lines of trucks with their trailers cross the desert carrying goods and supplies. Life is hard for the miners and their families but the pay is good and they have long holidays away from the desert.

▶ This is Mount Isa near Simpson Desert in Queensland, Australia. It is one of many iron, copper and lead mining towns around the Australian Desert. The metal ores are mined from the hills seen in the back of the picture.

Bringing water to the desert

▼ The land becomes fertile and plants grow when water is brought to the desert. This irrigator carries water across a strip of land. When one strip has been well watered the irrigator moves on.

Desert land can be made fertile by **irrigation**. This is a way of bringing water to dry lands so that crops and fruit can grow. Some countries have desert land and a lot of people to feed. This cannot be done without irrigation.

The ancient Egyptians used water from the River Nile to help their crops grow on the dry land on either side of the river. They built dams and dug ditches. They found ways of lifting the water and guiding it to the land where it was needed.

Irrigation today

Irrigation is mainly used where rivers flow near or through desert land. Huge dams have been built across the Nile, the Colorado River in the United States and the Murray River in Australia. Where there is plenty of water some of it is kept back in **reservoirs**. The water is carried in pipes or channels to the land where it is needed. The water has to be spread evenly over the dry land. It is pumped along small pipes and sprayed on the ground by **sprinklers**.

Sometimes very long pipes with sprinklers are used which go very slowly round in a circle. This way the water is always falling on the land. Huge circles of crops grow in the desert where this method is used.

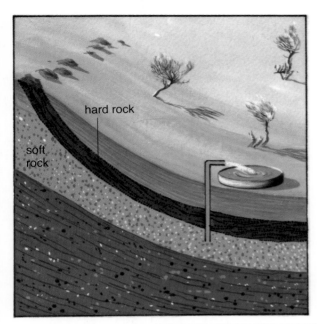

hard rock

soft rock

Underground water

Sometimes water for the desert comes from the **water table** under the ground. It comes to the surface at an oasis or at a water hole. In other places the water table is much deeper. When a deep well is dug, if the water is under **pressure**, it gushes out. This is called an **Artesian well**. These wells are used a lot in the Australian Desert.

Using sea water

Some countries like Saudi Arabia use sea water to irrigate their desert land. The salt must be taken out of the water first. This costs a lot of money. Some countries are able to use money from the oil they sell to pay for this way of making fresh water.

▲ In some dry parts of the world, water lies deep under the Earth. It is trapped under layers of hard rock. An Artesian well can be bored through the hard rock. Then the water in the soft rock comes up to the surface.

► This picture was taken from a plane. It shows a farm in Texas, USA. The irrigator is a long arm which moves around in a circle. A large circle of land is watered and the crops can grow well.

Oil from the desert

▼ Kuwait City has been built on land which was once desert. Near the city are oilfields. They supply the world with much of its oil.

drilling rig

hard rock

gas

oil

water   water

Oil and natural gas are trapped in layers of soft rock, under layers of hard rock. A hole is drilled down through the hard rock so that oil or gas can be brought to the surface.

Oil is made from tiny plants and animals which once lived in the sea. Some 300 million years ago, many desert lands were covered by shallow seas. When the tiny plants and animals died, they sank to the floor of the sea. They were buried in mud and sand. The mud hardened and was pressed down by new layers of mud and sand. The tiny plants and animals trapped inside the rock turned into little drops of oil. This took millions of years to happen. Oil has now been discovered deep under many of the world's hot and cold deserts.

Drilling for oil

Deep holes are drilled into the ground to find oil. The drill is held in a tall metal frame called a **drilling-rig**. The end of the drill is called the **drill-bit**. There are different sorts of drill-bits. Each one drills best through a particular kind of rock.

When oil is found, it is forced by pressure to the surface. Sometimes it is pumped from the desert along pipelines to the coast. The oil is then taken from the coast in ships called tankers, to many parts of the world.

Oil from the Arab world

Nearly half the world's oil comes from the Arab states in North Africa and the Middle East. Small countries, like Kuwait, who have found oil in their desert lands have become rich. Oil is needed by countries who do not have enough oil of their own. These countries are prepared to pay high prices to those who have oil. Oil is sometimes called 'black gold'.

The world uses millions of tonnes of oil every year. One day all the world's oil will be used up. It is difficult to think of life without oil. We use oil in our cars, to heat our homes and to make power for **factories**.

Change

The lives of many desert people change when oil is discovered. New towns are built. The money from oil pays for schools, roads, houses and factories. Many desert people give up their nomadic life to work on the oilfields. Some go to live in the new towns.

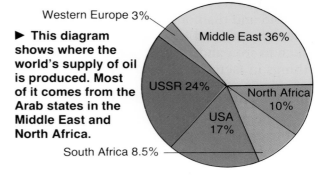

► **This diagram shows where the world's supply of oil is produced. Most of it comes from the Arab states in the Middle East and North Africa.**

Western Europe 3%
Middle East 36%
USSR 24%
North Africa 10%
USA 17%
South Africa 8.5%

▼ **This picture shows a small oilfield in the desert. It is near Dubai, a state on The Gulf. The drilling-rig stands high above the desert.**

Minerals of the desert

The waste lands of the world are rich in minerals. Minerals are stones, metals and various kinds of salt. Some of them, such as gold and diamonds, are valuable because they are rare and hard to find. Others, such as iron and copper, are used to make things in factories all over the world.

The salts of the deserts

Some minerals are found on the surface of the desert because they have not been washed away by the rain. The Atacama Desert of South America is rich in **nitrates**. These are used on the land as **fertilizers** to make plants grow well.

Huge **deposits** of salt lie on the surface of the Sahara Desert and the Great American Desert. They are all that is left of old salt lakes which have dried up in the sun.

Rare metals and stones

Gold and silver are precious metals. People have looked for these in the waste lands for hundreds of years. They have been used to make coins and jewellery since very early times.

▲ Opals are precious stones which are used in jewellery. They are found in rocks in the Australian Desert. The people who search for them have to break through the hard rock to find the opals.

Gold used to be found on the surface of deserts in the days of the Gold Rushes of the United States and Australia. Gold dust and small pieces of gold were washed downstream from the mountains. Now it is mined in South Africa and the cold waste lands of the USSR.

Minerals of the waste lands						
Deserts	Diamonds	Precious metals	Iron metals	Copper	Other metals	Chemicals
Arabian						●
Atacama			●	●	●	●
Australian		●	●	●	●	
Great American		●	●	●	●	●
Iranian			●			
Kalahari and Namib	●		●	●	●	
Patagonian			●	●	●	
Polar	●	●	●	●	●	●
Sahara			●	●	●	●
Takla Makan and Gobi			●	●	●	
Thar			●		●	
Turkestan		●	●	●	●	

Diamonds and opals are precious stones. They are used for jewellery. Diamonds are very hard, so they can also be used for making sharp cutting tools. The tools are used for drilling through hard rocks and metals. Diamonds are found in the Kalahari and Namib Deserts in southern Africa. Opals, which shine with many colours, are mined in the rocks of the Australian Desert.

Useful metals

Steel is used to make many things, from machines to knives. It is made from iron **ore**. The ore is a rock that has grains of iron in it. There are now huge iron mines in the Australian Desert. The Atacama Desert and the Great American Desert are rich in copper. This metal is used for making wires and pipes.

Bauxite (*bork-zite*) is used to make a metal called aluminium. This light metal is used for making window frames and parts for cars and planes. Like many other useful minerals, bauxite is found in many of the world's waste lands.

▼ Niger is a country to the south of the Sahara Desert. In some parts of Niger, tin is found near the surface in the sandy soil. The tin is sifted from the sand. This is called 'panning'.

Working in cold lands

The cold waste land of Alaska is rich in oil and people go there to work. In winter it is dark for eight weeks and then the temperature can drop to −57°C.

When oil was found, a huge pipeline had to be built to carry the oil to the sea. This was one of the hardest jobs ever carried out in the Arctic. The Trans-Alaskan pipeline is 1300 km long. Half of the pipeline was built on stilts above the ground. Several kilometres were buried beneath the frozen ground so that the herds of caribou could move freely. While the pipeline was being built, lengths of pipe had to be brought over the frozen land by huge snow tractors.

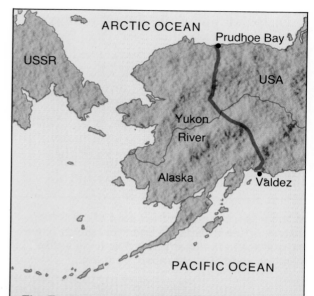

The Trans-Alaskan Pipeline was built to carry oil from Prudhoe Bay on the Arctic coast to Valdez on the Pacific coast. It crosses three mountain ranges and 600 streams and rivers.

◀ This picture shows a team of men working on the Trans-Alaskan pipeline. Heavy mobile cranes had to be used for lifting parts of the pipeline.

▶ There are many weather stations on the ice-cap. These people are visiting one on skidoos. They take readings of wind speed and the temperature.

The Inuit

Oil and minerals may bring wealth to the Inuit and the other people of the Arctic waste lands. It is certainly changing their nomadic way of life.

The Inuit have lived in the Arctic for thousands of years. They know how to survive the extreme cold. When they were nomadic hunters, the Inuit made their clothes with layers of animal fur. Their boots were made of sealskin. They made trousers from caribou and bearskin and undershirts of fur. Today most Inuit people buy their clothes from small shops or trading posts.

Homes

At one time the Inuit lived as nomads. They made snow houses, or used tents made of skin. Most of them now live in wooden houses at village settlements.

In Alaska, a large amount of money was spent on these settlements. New houses and schools were built. Today there is very little work for the Inuit people. Some of them can find work building roads around the mines and oil wells. The older men and women wonder if the young people who are now going to school will stay on the settlements or will have to leave to find work elsewhere.

The growing desert

Every year some deserts in the world grow a little bigger. This happens for several reasons. The land around the deserts is usually semi-desert. There is enough rain for some plants to grow and for animals to graze.

If this land is grazed by too many animals, the grass may not grow again. Where there are no plants to protect the soil, it is easily washed away by wind and rainstorms. The land then becomes desert.

This can also happen where people chop down trees for firewood or to make room to grow crops.

Herding animals

In the semi-desert, nomadic people move from one water-hole to another with their animals. At each stop, the sheep and cattle eat what grass they can find. Goats and camels are sometimes moved on to land where the **vegetation** has become very poor. Goats eat roots and shrubs. They can strip the land bare of all plants. If this happens, grass may never grow again and new desert is made.

Nomadic herders can make good use of land that might be empty waste land. New

◄ Goats damage semi-desert land more than any other animal. They even climb trees to feed on the leaves and the juicy stems. Then the trees die and the desert takes over.

► In the semi-desert to the north of the Sahara, people keep herds of goats on the mountain farms. Here the goats have overgrazed the land which will soon become desert.

water-holes and ponds can be dug to make larger grazing areas. The animals then need not eat all the grass in one place. They can move on to a new water-hole. This gives the grass time to grow again. The grazing needs to be controlled. The herds of animals must not grow too large.

Dust bowls

Some land is best used for grazing. Where this sort of land has been ploughed up to grow crops, dust bowls can develop. This happened on the grassy plains of North America and Australia.

In Oklahoma in the United States in the 1930s, farmers decided to grow more crops. They ploughed up vast areas of grassland. The grass had protected the soil. Its roots held the earth together. When there was a drought, the crops did not grow. The soil dried to dust. It was blown away by the wind. It can take many years and a lot of money to **reclaim** such land and make it fertile again.

▲ The Thar Desert is in north-west India. Around the water-hole you can see sheep, goats, cattle and a camel. There is very little food for these animals in the dry, stony desert. They soon strip the land of vegetation.

Disaster

▼ This map shows the world's worst disaster area. It stretches across Africa from west to east. Millions of people try to survive here as nomadic herders. There is very little rain. Sometimes there are long droughts with no rain at all.

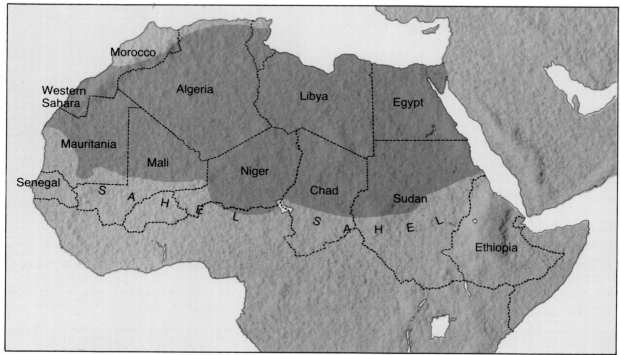

Many places in the world near to deserts are affected by drought. If the drought is very bad, many people may die. South of the Sahara is the semi-desert region of the Sahel. Usually there is just enough water there for nomadic herders to live and graze their animals. A drought which lasted nearly four years led to **disaster**. There was so little rain, the land became desert. Millions of animals and 250 000 people died.

Drought in recent years has brought disaster to parts of Ethiopia and the Sudan. Most people who live in Ethiopia are farmers. They grow crops for food and keep some animals to plough the land. There has been little rain for several years and the crops have failed. People have lived for months with very little food. Many have died.

Starvation

We need the right amount of food and water every day to keep well and healthy. In many parts of the world, people do not have enough food to live on. They can survive for a time but they are **undernourished**. They become weak and ill. Many people die from illness or lack of food. Children and old people are often the first to suffer. The effects of a famine can last a long time. Those people who survive may never become strong and healthy.

Sending help

Many countries and people who work for CARE, Oxfam and the Save the Children Fund have raised money to send help or **famine relief**. Sometimes it is too late to save people's lives.

There are several kinds of famine relief. First of all food, transport, medical help and fresh water are needed. Feeding and medical centres are set up. In Ethiopia many people were already too ill and weak to reach these centres.

When the drought is over, help is needed to get people back to their villages so that they can grow their own food again. The people need seed and animals, so that they can farm their land.

Lastly, help is needed to stop the famine happening again. New wells and irrigation can help to hold back the desert and improve the land.

▶ These children live in the semi-desert region of the Sahel. They are badly under-nourished. Each day they come to get extra food from an aid centre.

▼ In the heart of the Sahel semi-desert, cattle die from lack of water. Even after the first rains for years, there is hardly any water in this desert pool.

The future

The **population** of the world is growing. In a hundred years time there may be twice as many people on Earth. All these people will need food.

Any land that can be used to grow crops must be put to good use. Irrigation can be used, so that more crops can be grown on semi-desert land. Cheaper ways must be found to take the salt from sea water so that water can be piped to the desert.

People are now trying to find out how to grow plants without soil. One day, crops may be grown in the desert using the sun, minerals and water from the sea.

Ways of living

Finding oil and minerals in the world's deserts has given people who lived there a choice in the way they live. Many nomadic people have given up their old way of life. Some find work in the towns or in the oilfields or mines. For the Aborigines and Inuit, who live in settlements, finding work is often a problem. Many of the Bedouin have moved to the towns. Once all these people were nomads. Now some of them are trying to keep what is left of their old ways and pass their skills on to their children.

▼ This picture shows a small Inuit settlement in Alaska. The people now live in wooden huts. If they need help, or a doctor, a plane can come quickly to the settlement. The planes are fitted with skis for taking off and landing on the snow.

▶ Oil has brought wealth to many Arab states in the last 30 years. Kuwait has used some of this wealth to provide free schooling. These students are in the middle of a language lesson. Some of them will go on to university when they leave school.

The balance

How can we make best use of the world's deserts without harming them? Many of the world's waste lands are the homes of rare plants and animals. They are part of our **heritage**. We need the minerals and oil from the deserts and we need to use the deserts to produce more food.

Nomadic people have lived in the waste lands for hundreds of years without destroying the desert lands. What can we learn from them? They needed the desert to survive. They understood how to take just enough to live and to allow the wildlife around them to survive as well.

The future of the world's waste lands is still uncertain. Will we be able to take more and more minerals and food from the desert and let the wildlife survive?

▶ For hundreds of years, desert people have come to this market in Morocco. Most of them no longer wear their desert robes. They wear clothing bought in the market. Brightly coloured spices are also on sale.

Glossary

Aborigine: the name given to the first people to live in Australia. It comes from a Latin name meaning 'from the beginning'

adapt: to change in order to suit different surroundings

Artesian well: a deep hole in the ground, out of which water gushes

barrier: something that keeps people or animals apart

belt: a long continuous strip of land

canyon: a narrow valley with steep cliffs. Canyons are usually formed by rivers

caravan: a group of people and their camels travelling across the desert. They are usually carrying goods to sell

cattle station: a huge ranch or farm in Australia on which cattle are raised to produce beef

cold-blooded: describes animals which cannot make their own heat. Their bodies are hot or cold depending on the weather

continent: a large mass of land, sometimes including many countries. The Earth is divided into seven continents

deposit: something that is laid down or left behind on the surface

disaster: an event which causes great distress and loss of life

dissolve: to melt or break up

dormant: a state of not being in action, or sleeping

drill-bit: the end of the drill, used for grinding through the rock when drilling for oil

drilling-rig: the large metal structure which holds a drill

drought: a long time without rain

dune: a hill of sand built up by the wind

erode: to wear away the land by ice, water or wind

factory: a building where goods are made

famine relief: help given to people who are suffering from lack of food

felt: a kind of thick cloth made by pressing hair or wool flat

fertile: describes rich soil where seeds and plants can grow well

fertilizer: a substance that is added to the soil to make plants and crops grow well

fibre: the thread-like parts of a plant or tree

heritage: something precious which comes to us from the past

hostile: unfriendly

Ice Age: a time when much of the northern half of the Earth was covered by ice so that few things could live

ice-cap: a large mass of snow and ice. There is an ice-cap around the North Pole and the South Pole

industry: the work to do with the making or producing of goods, often in a factory

irrigation: a way of bringing water by pipe or river, to land that has little rain. Crops can grow on irrigated land

landscape: a wide view of an area of land. What the land looks like

larva: the second stage in the life of an insect. The larva hatches out of an egg

lichen: a slow-growing hardy plant that can live on very little food and water. Lichens grow mostly on trees and rocks

marsupial: a mammal which has a pouch on the outside of its body. The young develop in the pouch

mineral: any material dug from the earth by mining. Gold, coal and diamonds are minerals

moisture: water that is present in the air in tiny drops

moss: small thick plants with thin roots that grow on rocks and on marshy ground

nitrate: a substance which is added to the soil to help plants grow more quickly

nomads: people who move around from place to place and do not make their homes in one particular place

oasis: a place in the desert where water comes to the surface and plants can grow

ore: any rock from which metals can be taken

pack ice: large pieces of floating ice that drift around in the sea

pelt: the thick fur and skin of an animal

permafrost: soil beneath the surface that is frozen all the time

plankton: tiny animals and plants which float near the surface of the seas, oceans and inland waters. Plankton is a source of food for many water animals

population: the total number of people in a country or in one place

possession: a thing that is owned or kept

predator: an animal which lives by hunting and eating other animals

pressure: the action of one thing pressing on or against something else

prospector: someone who looks for gold or other minerals

quartz: a hard, very common substance found in rocks. Sand is made of tiny pieces of quartz

rain shadow: an area of little rain on the side of a mountain furthest from the sea

reclaim: to make waste land useful again

reservoir: a very large tank or lake where water is collected and stored

sap: an important liquid found in plants and trees which keeps them alive. Sap is rich in sugar

scrub: low bushes and small trees which grow on dry land

semi-desert: land which is dry most of the time, but has just enough rain for some plants to grow

sprinkler: a container with small holes which sprays water in small drops over plants

succulent: a juicy plant, such as a cactus, that stores water in its stem and leaves

temperature: the measure of heat or cold. How hot or cold something is

tundra: the cold, treeless plains of the north Arctic regions

under-nourished: not having enough food to keep healthy and grow properly

valley: low-lying land between hills

vegetation: all the plant or vegetable growth in a place

wadi: a dry valley or river bed in a desert. When it rains a wadi fills very quickly with water

warm-blooded: describes an animal that can keep its body heat steady. It does so by making its own heat. It can lose heat if it gets too hot

water table: the level below the ground at which water settles

yurt: a round tent made from fur and skin. Yurts are used by the Mongols in the Gobi Desert

Index